THE POETRY OF PRONOUNS

SHE. HE. THEY.

RICHARD M. ANKERS
GINA MARIA MANCHEGO

Copyright (C) 2023 Richard M. Ankers, Gina Maria Manchego

Layout design and Copyright (C) 2023 by Next Chapter

Published 2023 by Next Chapter

Cover art by Lordan June Pinote

Mass Market Paperback Edition

All rights reserved. No part of this book may be reproduced or transmitted in any form or by any means, electronic or mechanical, including photocopying, recording, or by any information storage and retrieval system, without the author's permission.

Gina
To he who has breathed life into my writing and into my heart.

Richard
To the only person I could dedicate this to: See Above.

CONTENTS

Foreword   vii

Part I
BEGINNINGS

She – Tuck Away	3
He – Indistinct	4
She – Chosen Reality	6
He – Daily	8
She – Courier Carbonation	10
They – In Utero	11
He – The Girl	12
She – Musings	14
He – Her Smile	15

Part II
TIME AFTER TIME

She – Counting	19
He – 7 Hours	21
She – Time Enough	23
He – Each Morning Brings the Sun	24
She – Borders of the Pane	26
He – Leapfrogging	28
She – Time Traveller's Wife	29
He – Seppuku	30
She – Petal's Pages	32
He – How to Explain?	33
She – Lightyear Surfing	35
He – Cobwebs	36
She – Love Adjacent	37
He – Every Time	39

Part III
DREAMS

She – The Moors	43
He – Moonstone	45
She – Thinking Out Loud	47
He – Silhouette	49

She – Open Spaces	50
He – Somewhere Between	52
She – Thistle and ONE	53
He – The Alchemist	55
She – Dream Worth Chasing	56
He – Seeing Rainbows	57
They – She and He in the Sky	58

Part IV
MELANCHOLY

She – Melancholia's Muse	61
He – Ghosting	63
She – Talk of Nonsense	64
He – Broken Mirrors	65
She – He	66
He – The Daylight Girl	68
She – The Point of No Return	70
He – Gothic	71
She – Ring	72
He – Silhouettes	74
They – The Sting	75

Part V
DOUBT

She – Deliverance	79
He – Away	81
She – Scales	82
He – Damson Tears	84
She – Binding and Ink	85
He – Is?	87

Part VI
LUST

She – Edging	91
He – Drip	92
She – Fruits	94
He – Skin on Skin	95
She – Cognac	96
He – Wild	98
She – In Black	100
He – Smoke and Mirrors	101

She – Underground Rave	102
He – She Breaks	103
She – Honey Dripping	104
He – Rorschach	106
She – Nature	107
He – Entwined	108
They – Peas	109
They – Fully Immersed	110
They – Mathamagics	111

Part VII
LONGING

She – My Darling	115
He – Come to Me	116
She – Classic Red Lipstick	117
He – Close Enough to Touch	118
She – Who is He?	120
He – Her Architecture	121
She – Water Sports	122
He – Frosted Flower	123
She – Skin	124
He – Aqualung	125
She – Twinkling Lights	127
He – Almost	128
They – Skin on Skin	129

Part VIII
HOPES & POSSIBILITIES

They - Other Worlds	133
They – Generational	139
They – Forever	145
She – Butterfly	146
He – You Found Me	148
She – Perennial Love	149
He – This Soul	150
She – You Tell Me	151
He – Small Spaces	153
They – Tissue Paper Hearts	154
They – 8th New Wonder of the World	156
They – A Question Tucked Away	158
They – Afterword	160

About the Authors

FOREWORD

"Every story has a beginning. Every day has its own page. Fate decrees much of this, the sun and the moon, too. The endings, however? Now, these we make for ourselves."

PART I

BEGINNINGS

"A story must know where to begin, from when to form the basis of all else. Theirs began with a letter tucked behind eyes that could not meet for fear of ruining a friendship. How was she to know? How was he? Bravery demanded this revealing and decreed that more would follow, much more. Yet in all beginnings a delicate touch is required, and they were no different to anyone else."

SHE – TUCK AWAY

Caught up in countless minutes of distant continental conversation.
There is beautiful bliss in finally being understood and seen.
Known and accepted for every part of me, not just the 'smoke and mirrors' beauty:
I scold myself for jeopardizing everything.
The days divide into ruminating riddles, as I attempt to place the exact moment his laughter became symphonic fragments of kaleidoscope light.
Was there a specific hour our friendship turned to this fire in my heart?
I've tried to pinpoint when I started to treasure the apples of his cheeks. What second of which month did I memorize the bends of his crow's feet? Each line, tiny little roadmaps to my daily joy.
This adoration for him is pure and perfect, like children twirling in the snow. The most pristine kind of love is sacrifice, me letting it go. Allowing it to melt into logic.
I tuck away the longing, the hope, the wishes. My feelings folded politely like a kerchief in the formal pocket suit he wore on his wedding day. What else can I do but smile and thank God he's my friend, because his happiness is all that matters in the end.

HE – INDISTINCT

BY TWILIGHT

Indistinct, she hovers at the periphery of my mind. I say mind and not eyes, for a person needs no eyes to love. You feel them, hear them, sense their presence with every atom of your heart and soul. You may flounder like a fish out of water but never quite drown as they engulf you. It becomes hard to breathe, every inhalation and exhalation catching in your throat. Who knew oxygen was made in her name? Who knew everything was made in her name?

BY NIGHT

I see her with her ink-black hair, a deeper shade of dream. Every time I stop to sleep, she's smiling. Every time I stop to weep, she's wiping the tears away. She pours across my body, a soothing balm. I'm so grateful, so humbled, so very much in pain. She tantalises with her spectral presence, so near, so far, so faint. The truth is, I'm in love with this ghost, and I'd die for her if it guaranteed our shimmering together.

BY DAWN

The amber glow of her skin illuminates. My waking life twitches to her nearness, her almost being here. Those eyes have changed since last I imagined them, sometimes hazel, sometimes brown, sometimes green. I study them like I might a kite flying through the sky. She, like it, is tethered too far from my fingertips. Still, I see her. I will always see her. That counts for something, doesn't it?

BY DAY

I bask in her beauty as I bask in her brain. She delights. To have found an angel of my very own, only to see her wings clipped and folded. This is the dilemma of those in love: To fly or to not? A golden prairie reflects in her window, sometimes covered by snow. I know the hooting owl watches over her, but what I'd give to live in his tree. I shall wait whilst the sun rises to its zenith and slowly dips away, thinking only of her, always of her, whilst my own pathetic life ebbs away. Indistinct, but lovely, she fades into another day.

SHE – CHOSEN REALITY

He is torn between real time and me. He laments about the distance and the world he settled into long before I existed. I see him trying to ride down a landslide of 'what if's' every-time the dichotomy doldrums set in.

It ebbs in him every day, he knows he's outgrown his skin. My man is caught in history's loop of obligation, the same day played over and again.

My Darling…wipe your tears, smile for me. Our love *IS* the reality, it's the only variable of this earthly plane that makes perfect sense.

Those dragging minutes that bleed into twenty-four-hour shifts are inconsequential acts. We are merely players in these roles we were born into. Autopilot performers going through what we accepted, long before we found ourselves in each other.

You and I are the chosen reality. This haven we've created is impermeable, a fortress so strong that it can't be eroded by miles, months, or incumbency.

My Love...do not weep and think of cruelty or a future marred by past decisions made. Instead, stand your ground, protect this pristine adoration from the ravages of the outside tempest. Be with me...in this dream. Let the rest fade away. 'Tis the only thing we can do, when you live in the real world of 'have to.'

HE – DAILY

Dawn
I saw the dawn rise in her eyes
as hope rose in her heart.
Her cheeks flushed, lips swelled,
skin glistened, like a misted meadow.
A darkness lifted from her
like a thin, satin sheet eased aside.
She shone for me, then,
my angel,
as she will always shine.

Midday
I see her as a tenuous dewdrop
Born of the morning,
Gone by midday.
She glistens through the darkness,
Striking, intelligent, bold,
This girl I've only ever wished well for,
A dream I long to hold.

Night

Do our shadows entwine in deepest night,
Writhe like reflections set free by the moon,
Slide over surfaces as dark as dead stars,
Slip through cracks from twilight 'til dawn?
Ebon misfits born from midnight's bell
Searching, questing, looking for something
All those illuminated others will never see.
Our lot, to ceaselessly wander the gossamer byways,
Not hand in hand, but forever soul on soul.

SHE – COURIER CARBONATION

What do you see when you look at me?

You smile like you're witnessing Christmas for the first time. A childlike wonderment, a bliss dancing in your eyes. Maybe I'm like the cathedral kaleidoscope prisms in your past. Do you see slivers of our eighteen months, or are you looking into the future?

What do you feel when you look at me?

The nervous anticipation before our minds meet of a hummingbird's wings flitting in your chest. Do you count the minutes before my eyes flutter like feathers? I wake and think of you.

The lady stirs.

Seconds seem like hours before our lifelines connect. Then effervescence, like the bubbles of Dandelion and Burdock overflowing and dancing on your lips.

'I love you baby.'

Sentiments fizzy and lighter than air, courier carbonation delivering me to you.

THEY – IN UTERO

Before life inhabited this planet
before the trees grew
before the flower stretched petals toward the sun
Before seasons of remembrance
And reasons to forget.
Before *the two* ever existed
There was still *Them*.
Incubating stardust atoms
In the vast black utero of space
One cell split in two.
Twin existence with one soul.

HE – THE GIRL

I see the girl in her coy smile,
the innocence dripping from her lips.
I see the sparkle in her hazel eyes,
as the fluttering lashes dip.

I see the facade drop there and then,
the game of life and its changes.
I see her lost in fractal pleasures,
the difference in how her mind ranges.

I see time shift from lines and stresses,
to porcelain perfection smoother than cream.
I see and feel how I seek to extend her,
from behind our glass-divided dream.

I see her always etched upon these aging eyes,
　imprinted upon my retinas for all eternity.
I see the girl, the woman, the angel, the joy,
　forever grateful of her seeing me.

SHE – MUSINGS

I already love your scenery.
Every morning I study the topography of your lines.
Whilst you lay in the curtained shadows.
Every morning I watch the golden dawn slide across
your skin like my own personal summer.
Everything about you is divine, and golden and
beautiful.
Perhaps we make each other beautiful.
Yes, my love, we are each other's beautiful.

HE – HER SMILE

It starts at the eyes, an uncontrollable narrowing,
like a joyous Cleopatra freed from obligation,
the desert taking on new clarity, oceans of sand,
the mysteries of the universe encapsulated in a
    hazel view.

There's a freedom in how her cheekbones lift,
    high and defined,
daring the greatest sculptor to mould superior
    perfection,
the taut, warm marble of her skin, polished and
    pure,
stretching to near translucent; rose tints rising.

Only then do those kissing lips twitch a worldly
    stutter,
following tugged lines of joy into the
    stratosphere,
revealing teeth that gleam with sheer undiluted
    pleasure.
They are contagious, these explosions of joy.

A man might do anything to see them never fade
 from her
celestial features, to pile such exquisite ecstasy
 there,
heap the happiness upon her.
I know I would. I can't live without her smile.

PART II

TIME AFTER TIME

"Time: The biggest obstacle of all. Time is the wrench thrown in life's spokes, the moments and fractions of seconds that divide our existences. Do we live the same sunrises? Do we like the same moons? By the time we form the questions, life has moved on."

"How does love conquer such restrictions? How do two become one when it's too dark to see the calculations? The answer: Breathe, breathe, and breathe again."

SHE – COUNTING

On the nights that sleep eludes me, I feel the familiar discourse rev up in my stomach.
10:39
Do the math: 5:39 in the morning when you rise. Are you rested? Did you have good dreams? Will you tell me you love me later when we meet through this battery powered partition? Do you mean all the wonderful things you say?
The questions roll in my mind, like worn out tires on lonely highways. I tread lightly because there's no tread left to spare.
My Love...I want to lose control of the wheel that steers my logic, and wreck into your mundane things.
Can I glimpse you getting out of the shower?
Wet, cream and sugar skin.
I long to be the condensation rolling down your pelvic bones. It's the only way I could be close enough to all that I need.
May I watch you put your clothes on, in the order you set them out the night before? Would you protest if I took them right back off your beautiful body?
I want to crash into you at full speed, send you reeling, give you amnesia about your past...so the only thoughts you have is of me, us, right now.

11:08
You drive home the sentiment, that you think of me in every second of your day. Even if that were true, it couldn't be more than I think of you, doing the ordinary things.
Which hand stirs the honey in your tea?
11:23

HE – 7 HOURS

The day begins seven hours after waking.
Inconsequential seconds have passed.
Seconds have entwined,
snaked their way into minutes.

    Minutes have drawn out to an eternity without you.
        These moments between being and not,
    these are the hardest. A delicious temptation,
    your presence teases what might or might not,
    as the static remains and the emotionless,
    cerulean skies show no signs of change.

Seven hours, I've counted every fraction of each.
The incessant buzz from ears which wish only to hear your voice.
seek to turn my mind, but my mind remains focused.
I'm counting off the seconds.
Can you hear me?

    There is no exact moment, just 'a' moment.
That moment is near, for my stomach churns and skin prickles.
I no longer watch the sky, listen to the static, or even count,

I just prepare. The seven-hour wait is almost over.
How I fear the next.

SHE – TIME ENOUGH

Make me yours in this ether, the place of secret dreams.

Shake off your waking world obligations, and erase the day like tedious lessons on notebook pages...

My love...I while away the hours 'til merciful rest takes me. With heavy lids and a sparrow heart, I resolve to make us the last thought that delivers me into slumber. 'Tis the only place where I can feel you on my skin.

Discover me with gentle offerings and I will open for you like a flower. Ebb with me slowly under night's cover and let my body move beneath yours in the way fate and desire intended.

Kiss my flesh with your dark eyes alone, memorize every single imperfection on this face that lights up for only you. Connect my freckles with the pads of your fingers, outline the love constellations on the apples of my cheeks. We are Andromeda and Perseus, star-crossed lovers vowing to illuminate for one another for all eternity. Even then, it won't be time enough.

HE – EACH MORNING BRINGS THE SUN

Each morning I am blessed by golden light and soothing warmth. There are no seasonal adjustments required. All I need is the same sumptuous view.

They say angels live amongst us, guiding us, sweeping the evil aside. You won't know they're there; they just are. I know, though, and I even know what time my angel will appear.

Each morning brings the sun to a life mired in darkness. The tar pit stomach shall bubble, the granite heart melt, the dark eyes simmer in cobalt. It is a process of demystification, one I welcome.

They say the day begins at dawn, as ruby burns away black and tangerine takes over. We move the time twice a year, but nature doesn't know this, and my angel doesn't care: our time begins at midday.

Each morning they say a lot of things, but we say only one, and that requires no words nor colours nor proposals of time. We say it with smiles and sparkling eyes as we always have and will.

How I love the sun each morning no matter where or when that is.

SHE – BORDERS OF THE PANE

The day is stark and pensive.

The cats crouch by the window with lulling eyes, daydreaming that they're lions living beyond the borders of the pane. Caged by the brick and mortar of predictability.

I dare to dream the same.

Ways for my downy nightingale wings to lift me across the sea to you.

My love...the seconds are like years whilst you slumber, and I am left to my own thoughts. I stumble about inside my head like drunken night follies, fumbling for what could have been instead of what really is.

I made a lot of mistakes, fell for demon hearts with flowering faces, gave myself away to shame and regret until there was nothing left.

Of the pristine me.

Even though you seem to see me differently, this victim of circumstance can only offer you what's left of her soul with unclean hands.

My love...can I pretend that I'm not second best? I must confess that I wish it was I that you cradle against you, I want to hear your heart beating my name inside your chest.

Devotional morse code.

It will never be. Perhaps these wings can fly me into other dreams where we meet again and again. Wait for me there patiently, my love, fore it's the only place where you're more than just...

'a friend.'

HE – LEAPFROGGING

Leapfrogging through time and space,
Waiting for the hours to dissolve.
Trying to allay the seconds,
As we clash in the night.
Merging with you throughout every moment,
Sluicing through your veins.
Searching out everything,
Swimming through your galaxies.
Like a comet set free, exploring.
Knowing that soon, very soon,
But never soon enough,
Your eyes will be here, your lips.
And everything will feel better for a time.
Whilst we pause mid-leap in the air
And all else falls away.

SHE – TIME TRAVELLER'S WIFE

They were nothing more than time travellers,
finding remnants of one another
in life's accumulation of centuries gone by.
All they needed to do was look into each other's eyes
to see they existed together,
memories made laid days on end,
spent moments living and laughing,
eons as lovers and friends.
She was grateful her soul still remembered him,
amongst stages of world-weary strife.
Amidst millions of minutes, then to now,
always knowing she was the time traveller's wife.

HE – SEPPUKU

The seconds extend to hours, the hours to days.
I await her return as the flowers do the sun,
as the desert does the rain. And I wonder:
   What if?
A stomach churns. Legs grow weak. What have I
   become?
I see her clearly: hazel eyes ensconced behind
   tendril lashes,
raven hair aglow in darkness, skin as white as
   snow.
She hovers at the periphery like an apparition,
sent by the universe to haunt my eternal dreams.
I need her more than food, than water, than the
   atoms
that comprise my being. I yearn for her.
What if?
Seppuku, the Japanese call it, ritualistic death.
Would I? To see her one more time. To hear her
   laugh,
see her smile the smile of an angel, hear her
   breathe.
Or would it be in the not seeing her? Does she
   need proof?

The blade pauses somewhere near my abdomen every day at dawn.
One day, the sun will not rise, and the blade shall plunge.
I am an honourable man, I think! I would do this for her.
I would do anything for her. Anything.
Yes, anything.
But one thing I could not do, as the blade disappears within,
is feel the pain I ought. For the loss of her is greater.
And I would never feel such agony again.

SHE – PETAL'S PAGES

You wrote of me before I existed.
A muse of what seemed would only live in your imagination.
Born from your every whim, I am creation, a figment of ebon hair and galaxy eyes.
This flower brought to life upon Petal's Pages, breathe me in with verse and pen.
My love…Where will you take me next now that I'm body and flesh?
I'll be with you anywhere.
Let's go to coffee at dawn, sip me long and slow like you would your Americano.
You're always brilliant in my mornings.
Tell me of your days gone by, like history books tucked in schoolboy rucksacks.
I want to know all the things you keep buried deep within your stories.

HE – HOW TO EXPLAIN?

How do you explain the changing of a life. When there is no apparent beginning, just a seamless passage of exchanged thoughts, what then? Can you remember the second your heartbeat changed? Can you recall the moment your pupils dilated and never quite closed again?

There are instances in time that stick. A first hello. A celebratory whoop that dismissed technological inadequacies. There were the tears of genuine sadness that marked an emergency, the photo of her laid in a hospital bed, masked as ill. Shared embarrassments make turning points, but they explain little about the heart and soul.

Explanations take time to perfect. A man who likes to think needs that so the mouth which blurts out nonsense might say the right thing.

I must think. Yes, think.

Was it sharing the same songs, parallel paths, equalised traumas? Maybe a photograph, or a video made to illicit joy? A word? Words are good for many things.

I have thought and I still think now, but how to explain any of it remains elusive. Maybe another me in another time, another reality, another dimension where we've always simply *been* would do better. I am at a loss. So, as I always do, or try to, I tell the truth.

Breathe. Breathe. Breathe.

I cannot explain how much I love you, how much it hurts when you're gone, how my stomach twists and knots, how my head pounds and eyes water, how my soul aches. It simply does. You are all I have ever wanted. You are my everything.

So, have I explained? Maybe. Maybe not. Only time spent on shared pillows, shared seats, in shared views and in shared positions, counting out shared seconds and hours together will say whether I did well. But you'll get the chance, my darling, as I hope beyond all measure, will I.

SHE – LIGHTYEAR SURFING

Cuz I miss
when you're not talkin' to me
I be deep vibin' off our energy
I see
the colors in you. Amber, blue and green
No space between

65,700 minutes of 'we'
Light year surfing
Through this galaxy.

HE – COBWEBS

I see her as a cobweb, one I would share. To writhe in her gossamer embrace…ah, what bliss. To see the world through her eyes, hear through her ears, whilst dangling from an invisible chord. To lie with her and feel the wind tickle our life threads, to risk being devoured. True, cobwebs don't last forever, but what does other than the love which made them.

SHE – LOVE ADJACENT

We lay adjacent on my mornings, darting like fractal light playing hide and seek with reality.

He filters through the heavy curtains that once blocked out the world.

Draw back those sullen drapes of years past.

I let him in as I accept the dawn, I open myself to both.

We devote adjacent, like twins in the womb. Foreheads pressed together, as close as we can get without one becoming the other.

He and I speak of gratitude and despair for the glass cages of our digital telephone screens.

'Petal, can you hear my heartbeat?'

. . .

We lie adjacent, oblivion and obligation swallow up our minutes.

'Time is never time at all…'

Until we're left with the remains of the day.

Twenty-two hours between what's needed to sustain us.

Seven thousand-two hundred seconds together, is but a single raindrop in a desert with two people so thirsty for one another. We meet at the oasis of our union, lips parted in anticipation so we may drink in…

love, adjacent.

HE – EVERY TIME

Every time you breathe a word, I remember why I listen: To hear that which I want to scream.

Every time you blink a look, I remember why I watch: To see my reflection in your eyes.

Every time your skin reacts, I remember why I feel: To imagine your touch.

Every time we part, I remember why I love you: To feel less alone.

Every. Single. Time.

PART III

DREAMS

"Sometimes, dreams are all you have, all you know, all you want. Dreams exist to fill the blanks that life refuses. Some fear them. Some can't wait for sleep. Others aren't sure whether they're even dreaming at all."

SHE – THE MOORS

He delivered me softly down in the heather of the moors.
I rose and fell with him amongst amethyst flower sails billowing on the waves of our shared inhalations,
Like a lost love message rolled tightly in a stained-glass bottle, bobbing along heavy tides praying to be found.
He reads me.
In solemn reverence, I was memorized word for word as though scripture.
Only he could decipher between these lines to navigate the dark and lonely world inside.
My Love… How many lifetimes have your lips discovered my skin?
Tell me!
We are merely recycled relics, colliding in every eternity.
Name, address nor date bares consequence, fore our existence together doesn't answer to the riddles of minutes.
I knew your eyes for the first time again.
Mirrors of the steely mountains, the only home I've ever known.
Inside them I see traces of us and our reincarnated 'used to be.'

I'm caught up in your marrow, like a willing moth in a web.
Your language, your truth, the beauty, the sin.
It all weaves me in tight, like we are the same tapestry of stars.
Both radiating millions of light years from here.
Laid days on end spent sunbathing amongst the bend of your smile.
Galaxies floating in the supernova of your kiss, wading through centuries, whilst waiting to touch you.
My Love, I am ready to dance with you, like the hands whirl on my wristwatch, lead me into the next chapter of our infinity.
The moors stand silent again, bathed in lavender and love.

HE – MOONSTONE

1 - A celebration of celestial magics, where one becomes two, she penetrates this abyss. There is no intention to frighten, to terrorise the dormant heart. This night was never meant to contain.

2 - I dream of tendril hair that twists like kelp caught in tidal squalls. Of ultramarine lips that purse, perhaps in anticipation, perhaps in melancholy musings. Do the moonstones glow a little brighter, I frown? Has the universe dimmed? No. She has entered my liquidated self. This dream is recollection.

3 - The darkness contracts. Something stirs in ink black depths. A boulder blooms. A rock sheds its granite epidermis. The moonstones permeate more than ever did light. Oh, how her eyes stir this soul. I have a soul!

4 - I am still the darkness. Still the depths. Still wretched. But under her gaze there is hope. There is love. Is this how it felt in the beginning or only at the end? I forget. I have forgotten so much.

. . .

5 - The moonstones descend in gentle illuminations, and I know at last what once was the truth. There is no moon under which I brood. There is no sun from which I flinch. There is no ocean in which I drown, only her eyes. Those beguiling moonstone eyes. I await the rest, heart pounding.

SHE – THINKING OUT LOUD

Don't mind me...I'm just thinking out loud.
What if you would have met me first, would you love me the same?
What if you were younger or I were older? Could we have found a place to meet in the middle, would I have your last name?
I wonder.
My Love...If I were yours, I'd have been a good wife. In the beginning we would have been poor and perfect for each other, inhabiting a tiny flat. A mattress and one pillow to share; that penny-worth pallet would cradle us under the window.
The dawn would trickle in every morning and light up your beautiful face. After all, like the sun, my happiness rises in your smile.
We would have spent all our time on that bed island, surrounded by a sea of worn sheets. Our bodies moving together on cresting waves of contentment. We'd have taken turns scrawling love poems on each other's bodies with a single ball point pen. Authors bound together with ink and flesh.
And time would keep typing... You'd fill pages with words, growing chapters. I'd grow with the babies you'd fill me with, life would ebb in me like verses

being born in your novels. Our children would have been named after classic authors: Silvia, Brontë, Poe and William. They would scribe adventures in primary handwriting with crayons and sheets of paper. We'd have both been so proud that each kid's stories would be displayed on the refrigerator. Stuck on with magnet souvenirs of a life well lived. A family of writers painting beautiful scenes with each brush stroke sentence.

And time would keep typing… With the kids all gone we would've sat to watch the sunset on quiet evenings together. We'd talk about how we met all those decades ago. You'd tell me a joke and I'd pretend to hate it. Your arthritic fingers would have jotted a poem about how stunning I still was. You'd have written of my moonstone eyes and my ebon sails of hair; I'd blush and kiss your perfect lips.

If I'd had been your wife, I would've run your bath, put out your robe so you wouldn't catch a chill, folded down the covers on our bed. I would have made love to you one last glorious time, hearts pressed together as our final chapter came to an end.

But I wasn't first, it could never be…still, I can't help thinking out loud.

HE – SILHOUETTE

I see you in silhouette
A tantalising ghost
An outline of seduction
Awaiting to be filled
To be coloured in
To be made whole
Not intangible, vaporous
But a woman of solidity
No longer a dream
But my dream, fulfilled

SHE – OPEN SPACES

My wish?

That we were the only people in this expansive world.

Our love would protect us from the rages of time and catastrophe.

Exploration of each other and open spaces.

We'd run around in meadows of heather, naked and free.

If we were hungry, we'd pick apples off abundant trees. You'd let me feed you from thine own hand.

I'd give you sustenance with my body and mind.
Let us spread our wing and fly to the ends of the earth.
Larger than life.
'We are one!'
Our voices in unison would bounce along the terrains of the Grand Canyon.
Echoing off the walls like adoring melodies of resounding resonance.
'One'
'One'
'One'
The word would flood back over us, awash in reckoning.

We'd simply smile at each other, knowing from the first moment we met, we would never again be two.

HE – SOMEWHERE BETWEEN

Somewhere between the stars and eternity, she waits breath held, as celestial forces ease us together.

I'll find you.

Nebulous, a ghost to the love we hold, she's drifting just beyond my outstretched fingers.

Reach harder.

There is the universe, reality, if you will, and then her. She is all I see. She fills my vista.

Don't blink.

No lie is this. No false God has placed her. She's as real as the dream from which I dreamed her.

Hold tight.

Somewhere between the stars and eternity, she's crying, but not from sadness, from joy.

Together forever.

SHE – THISTLE AND ONE

Some girls are cute little blue belles dappling meadows on sunny days. They spring to life and blanket the earth like God smiled all the while, as he drizzled happy hues on earthly canvas.

Some women are elegant, Red Eden Roses. They stretch long stems toward the sky, blooming lux crowns, like flamenco dancers unfurling silk ripples of fragrant endearments.

Then there's me, I am the thistle.

'Nemo me impune lacessit.'

Under the duress of seasonal burden, the thistle has evolved thick, impermeable stock that doesn't bend under the trample of machine or beast. Leaves that do not crumble against the bitter winds of winter.

I find the will to stand back up even after one considers me crushed.

A thistle endures.

This thistle is barbed and harsh. Spines of milky poison, meant to pierce the skin of any man that dares comes near. I'll cut into your tender flesh, welt, and infect the very stream of blood coursing through your veins.

An arsenal of natural weaponry to keep me safe, keep intruders at bay.

All steer the course clear of me but ONE.

ONE fearless farm boy, despite the promise of pain and poison still comes to water me every day. This ONE is the nurturing a thistle needs.

Only he, the deserving ONE can see the glory in me. The ONE waiting patiently whilst I display a steadfast bloom. He looks upon me, this flower, like I'm the most precious thing he's ever seen. True love becomes beauty where all the others saw the weed.

HE – THE ALCHEMIST

Sprinkles of laughter and life.
The twist of a winking eye.
Shifting with the seasons.
Swimming golden tides.
The mysteries of forever.
Riddles played close to the heart.
A little bird whistles
To the great cat in the sky.
The stars blink out, snuffed.
Dancing beneath an ivory moon,
Reflection captured in ice.
Rituals practised for two.
The pause before the storm.
She thinks, waits, decides,
Eyes evoke, violin lips speak.
The alchemist has me
Curled around her heart.
I'm changing, changing,
And I'll never change back.

SHE – DREAM WORTH CHASING

I've never been much for hoping.
Life was quick with lessons about defeat.
I slipped, stumbled, knocked down too many times to remember.
You stop counting on punching-bag-promises.
And rope-a-dope riddles.
Wishes belonged to others. Never prayers asked for me.
I kept the expectations low, that way I wasn't disappointed for opportunities missed.
Nothing ventured, nothing gained.
Until we met…
You're the dream worth chasing.
4,500 miles, like the Proclaimers,
Just to be the one that falls down at your door.
I'd claw and crawl
And
Shout that you're the prize on the other side of the sea.
You and me.
This love is legend in the making.

HE – SEEING RAINBOWS

She sees rainbows in the air, whilst I gaze adoringly at her raven hair. This kaleidoscopic vision is just the first of many things we share.

The prairie always has rainbows, she says. *They're nothing extraordinary here.* But we don't. Until she smiles, that is, and rainbows reappear.

I see the world in colours, now. Her exuberant colours. And if God is willing and fate divines, I'll see rainbows as often as she, for there's no monochrome for lovers.

Seeing rainbows is a gift, I decree. Such natural majesty defies description. Just knowing they're there, however, means so much more to me.

THEY – SHE AND HE IN THE SKY

She and He in the Sky.

Their arcs run parallel, resting against heaven whilst taunting the earth.

Treasure hunters chase them to find their end, in search of riches and glory. They don't realize that it's the beauty that's the prize.

One bends to cradle the other, unending and glorious...this is their love.

PART IV

MELANCHOLY

"Dark minds think darker thoughts, deeper realms, abyssal truths; they seem too close. Hope seems further, possibility non-existent. Skies hang leaden and heavy. The air is thick. Here, every candle burns an ebony flame that casts myriad shadows. But they do burn, at least, and that's a start, for every lux of light begins as an ember."

SHE – MELANCHOLIA'S MUSE

Act Un
My man, in his madness, creates symphonies of lamentation with word.

He strings together dolefulness, like sullen syllables perched on pain.

Balancing the wire in storm and despair.

Scribing to please the reaper - 'tis better to make him a friend.

Offering verses of dismal deliverance, set up like pretty maids all in a row.

Lay the departed lines down, dressed in their Sunday best.

My man thinks if he writes it enough, it will be his emancipation from death.

Act Deux
I am Melancholia's muse!

Created from the recesses of his lonely heart, fore even the most sullen suitors need understanding.

I wear gossamer gowns made of shadows for him, twirling in the umbra, like plumes of smolder and smoke.

Flashing my brooding eyes his way, their haunting depths give him inspiration for prose.

Pages of morose poetry a day is how he pays the reaper.

I bare my dark soul and my pale flesh, while he pens of our love story.

So much like Poe and his darling Elmira.

Finir
It's the unwritten contract we have, us three.

My man Melancholia, the reaper and me.

HE – GHOSTING

We dream their faces,
Their translucent skin.
We imagine who they were,
What they did,
What they've done.
As ghosts they visit our dreams.
Creeping into those cavities of self,
We seek to hide from others.
They know us better than we know ourselves.
When the night comes,
We crave them.
In those moments of blue and grey,
They lie in the shadows, waiting,
Eyes blazing, lips pressed tight.
And we realise, then,
That the world is not full of ghosts,
Rather, it is we who are ghosting,
Waiting for the one who shall take the fear away.
Waiting for you, my love.
Guide me.
Let me know you.
Be the spirit that has always haunted this soul with kindness,
Because I never want to go to sleep alone again.

SHE – TALK OF NONSENSE

He and I lay together every day and talk of nonsense to past the time.

There's never anything much to say but we don't want to bid 'goodbye.'

I whisper:

"My Love, I hope I die first, fore I couldn't bear wandering through life alone. My heart would cease to beat without its home. It lives in you.

I see the tears well in his eyes. He blinks them back because stoic men don't cry.

He speaks over the lump in his throat:

"My Beauty, you never need worry, I'll forever hold you near. When I take my last breath, I won't harbor any fear. Your face will be the last thing I see.

I weep through words:

"My Love, but you don't believe in God, or a paradise in the sky. How can you promise we'll be together when we die?"

He smiles at me gently and utters:

"My Beauty, I know you'll go to heaven, all angels do…and that's where I'll be because my paradise is in you…

HE – BROKEN MIRRORS

Seen in the mirror each day, she shines
a mercury madness into these cobalt eyes:
How the quicksilver boils in this soul.

I tap upon the glass an incessant staccato,
hoping she hears, praying she knows:
An eyelash bats in my direction.

Like ice, cold and clear, the glistening surface
teases her,
like my own personal Mona Lisa:
Hang upon my wall and smile us a century.

When did desperation strike? When did the universe
declare us, *Us*? Whose heart beats the loudest? The
questions gush a waterfall:
Drown me. Please!

Broken mirrors reflect infinite faces, but all I see is
hers.
The cuts won't kill me, as our blood and histories
merge:
Dying together is better than living apart.

SHE - HE

Every day, he writes the wrongs for me...

Crafting poetic sermons in devotional tongue. His paragraphs paint me as an angel, sent to save him from the beige day blues.
He says my beauty is color in the clouds.

Where I am his heaven, he is my tree.
This man is sweet sanctuary, a steadfast oak.

Before 'us' I only knew the past.
Hard unforgiving ways, like a frantic fawn pulled into the current.
Breaking myself over jagged rocks.
Only treading as I became bloodied and bruised, hardly alive when I was delivered onto the banks.

Struggling and just surviving.

I thought "love" meant almost drowning, losing myself and being swept under.

Then he appeared, fatefully ready to save me.
This strong tree.
Knowing limbs, with deep, wise roots, he outstretches
wide arms welcoming me home to his heart.

He bends to protract his branches, lifeline leaves
rustling for my notice.
I grab for him, and he is unwavering as I pull myself
out of the dangerous waters.

My Love gives me shelter from the storm, an arbor
example of what a good man can be.

I lean on him and rest my weary soul.

At the very least I hope this poem will show my
appreciation for my darling oak tree.

Because every day, unconditionally, he *writes* the wrongs
for me.

HE – THE DAYLIGHT GIRL

She needed the daylight more than anyone. Her pale skin demanded light. Her eyes twinkled like stars, not reflecting the moon, but the sun. If ever a creature was born to walk God's pastures and meadows, smelling the flowers, and smiling at the rain, it was her. So why had they kept her locked in a room like a bird in a cage for longer than any prisoner? They didn't care, and never had.

She had taken lovers. They had flocked to her features like tourists before Lady Liberty. Fingers had pointed. Tongues had lolled. Not a one had asked her what she wanted. She knew them, of course. She served them up desires the likes only Scheherazade knew. They marvelled at her tongue and her delights.

These men took advantage of her wiles, never caring of the why she used them, or how. It was always them, not her. Always want. She got what they served, not ever what she deserved.

Her heart bloomed for a while. Youth does that. She shone like the Evening Star, blazing a trail through the sky, a veritable living Venus. When she smiled, they swooned. When she laughed, they suspected the worst. All she ever wanted was the truth. Was it so hard to find!

The years past in flashes of joy and wild moments; most meant little in the greater scheme. Fate served her a son, if not the father he deserved, and for this she felt blessed. But a mother is still a woman and all women, as in all people, have needs. These needs went unmet.

There were dalliances, of course, and more besides. Some lasted, or rather, were enforced. The shackles bound her tighter by the day, but she did not break. They could not break her. Would not. Until…

Life is hard and for her it was harder than most. Fear of violence does such things. She trembled like a snowdrop battered by the wind. She cowered through necessity, not want. As in all things, she endured.

Another came and then the supposed best, who was in fact, the worst. He hurt her so deep sadness polluted her soul. She turned from him with difficulty, choosing written words to cup her outpoured emotions. A talent. A skill. Someone noticed.

They talked about everything and anything. They laughed; it was nice to laugh, forgotten even. The two shared everything without fear of reprisal, judgement or worse. They were the same, you see, she and him.

Now she sits by her window, not hiding beneath the sheets. She watches the dawn rise in his eyes, as he does hers. Now, she walks in the world she once graced, step by step, bit by bit. He's so proud of what she's achieved and shall continue to. Theirs is a gentle love, one born of respect. Theirs is the sort of purity hearts were made for. Two souls conjoined, this is she and he.

Her life is only just beginning. Wait and see.

How do I know? How do I the narrator of this tale speak with such confidence. Ah, I'd tell you, but I'm watching the sun rise, and not in the sky.

SHE – THE POINT OF NO RETURN

My love... we're steps away from the point of no return.
This entanglement, I'd burn for it.
Would it be wise to stop now before it's too late?
You see, I hate the thought of your restlessness.
The kind in your eyes today.
I'd do anything to take it all away, but could I, if I tried?
I almost died of guilt when I realized your thoughts were of me,
Instead of seaside vacations with your tangible family.
Soon, land and circumstance will have us resenting the minutes of life we're not together.
My fear is that we'll weather the storm, batten down the hatches, ride out the waves,
Stave off this pain and deny the longing...
Until the day you determine I've become a stain on the clean perfect life you're used to.
Then what's to become of the 'me' that would die for you?

HE – GOTHIC

I spy her in this gothic dream
Tempestuously brooding, dangerous, dark
Her storm clouds tinting the horizon with indigo ink
And cursive lines
Her crashing waves devastating
Furious to behold in all her magnificence
She glowers through this ebon somewhere
Those eyes! Those eyes!

In kohl and cremation, she buries her suitors
But not me. Never me.
For the wolves call and bats descend
The nocturne stretching into infinity
All mist and fog and setting sun
To cloak our souls together, entwine
The ghosts of our rapture haunting forever
Beware! Beware!

SHE – RING

Each day he crafts me lines like he is polishing precious Jet from the Whitby sea,

Tumbling his words around and around like driftwood rolling against the shoreline.

His love makes even the cracked and splintering bits seem beautiful.

He's blind to the broken and bruised parts of this muse. The ravaged girl that was washed up on life's rocky coast. Only he recognized something precious in me.

I am his jewel, spinning and refining around and around in his head from dawn to dusk.

Does he know that the pieces of me in those poems are more valuable than anything I've ever owned?

. . .

I carry his verses with me like little baubles of Jet in an eternity ring.

'Til death do us part.'

...and even then, his poetry will welcome me into the hereafter.

HE – SILHOUETTES

Silhouettes
Mirroring darknesses
Where one resides
The other follows
Where one hides
The other squeezes in

                Silhouettes
                One to the other
                Ebony and onyx
                Obsidian to black
                Equals in eternity
                Shining dark lights

                              Silhouettes
                              Deeper than deep
                              No longer shadows
                              Pools of dark lights
                              But images
                              Of one another

THEY – THE STING

The sting hurts less each time as the storm clouds gather in cumulus anticipation. Who cares what the world says.

There are spaces of truth, reality, of a fashion, that infiltrate logic like pins in a balloon. Who cares what the universe expects.

The hurt diminishes because the joy overwhelms it. We win where others have failed. We're stung. Stung forever!

The clouds roll across the day to reaffirm the night's position: The stingers vanish into the shadows.

PART V

DOUBT

"Doubt is akin to fear as love is to hate. One without the other just isn't the same. We must be strong to overcome doubt, face it head on. We always think we've the strength to do so, but in reality…?"

SHE – DELIVERANCE

On angry occasions, your dad and my mom get into battles about who's right and who's guilty.

They lie in wait like demons looking for times of weakness. That is when the possession takes hold, we leave our bodies and float just above this molecular flesh.

Watching our mouths moving and fingers wagging.

Hypocrisy and blame escape through the bars of cell-block teeth. Wounding phrases that should be forever held in solitary confinement break free from relentless cages.

Where have *We* gone?

We bend almost until our backs break in this dirty tango, like willows in a squall.

Rage is easier than fear and longing.

With hoarse voices, we get the last words in before deciding to get out of the mess we made of love.

You wipe away at weeping eyes and ask that I look
upon the man who would die for me.

Deliverance back into myself.

I look at your face and know you've found your way
back too from this brim of desperation and insanity.
Life seizes us sometimes when loneliness, jealousy, and
logic are simply too much to bear.

HE – AWAY

The parting is hard,
The being parted, harder.
But there's always the return
To brighten grey days
And make us realise
Just what we were parted from,
Isn't there?

Click!

The screen goes blank.

SHE – SCALES

We try our best to balance out the days like shiny coins on delicate scales.
If one of us moves without the other in tandem, the liability of tipping and falling isn't far off.

...and we risk it all for this affair, even the plummet.

Desperate people collecting the debts of sin and desire, like bad deals made of pyramid scheme promises. You, me, she...a triad of misgivings.

Still, we can't stop pushing forward, buying precious moments whenever we can. Even when we've run out of spare change and time, we
IOU
seconds on the clock
with stories
with sweet talk
with sadness
and worries.

Oh, how we pay!
Heads or tails?
Consummation or longing?
Truth or loyalty?
Not a pence left to spare.

Yet we continue saving what little we have.
So, we don't dare offset the scales of this shiny coin
kind of love.

HE – DAMSON TEARS

Damson tears fall like bruised fruits,
Colouring the ground in pith and sadness,
Staining the world with dark sorrow.
Fruitless, these loving endeavours
Take a seasonal toll in minutes.
Yet, with time and patience, arboreal care,
Blossoms may bloom and ripen,
Shades of pink and hints of Spring.
But time is not availed to us, and sharp
Rains and acerbic winds shall usher
The damson tears again, a purple deluge.
This is our cycle, one of bruises.

SHE – BINDING AND INK

Pen these pages and keep them coming.
This labor of love.
Sentences flowing like tributaries into the collective consciousness of
You and I
Saying the same things in different flowering themes.
'I love you.' Over and again.
'What if?'
The prequel,
the present,
and of course, the epilogue.
Even if it is unknown.
We make ridiculous excuses about writing a book with our last names side by side on the cover.
For fame,
for glory,
for penny royalties.
None of it matters.
So why do we keep writing?
Has this distance between us caused us two scribes to go mad?
A frenzy of punctuated sentiments.
The glue holding what little time left we have of this life together.

When we're mostly apart.
That must be why we type 'til our fingers bleed and our eyes sting with knowing tears.
That the years will fly, the hellos and goodbyes will never be anything but brief.
The only thing we can navigate with this love are these poems.
'Us'
pressed tightly together by binding and ink.
Existence immortal.
Amongst these white paper sheets.

HE – IS?

Is she real, this girl of mine
This indescribable illusion
Built from dreams,
Sent from the stars to light the way
To steer this heavy heart
This caged soul released?
Is she realer than this reality
I seek to escape
In worlds built solely for her
An inter-dimensional ghost
Reoccurring beyond my fingertips
Over and over again?
My porcelain queen
Marbled in our colour
Deep blue like the wildest seas
Is she? Is she?
Because life's not worth living
If she's not
?

PART VI

LUST

"The inescapable reality of time spent without the other, this is the habitat in which lust resides, always wanting, always needing, always wating for more. In lust are emotions most betrayed and, worst of all, hidden."

SHE – EDGING

I watched him today, in an exquisite state of euphoric revelation. He declared his love for me, not with poem but with staggered breath.

The heavy air escaped his lungs, like a wild horse running toward a deep ravine. Urgent exhalation followed closer as he raced toward ecstasy. The longer he traversed the aching center of himself, the less he cared about life or death. He was willing to plunge over the brim of the unknown if it meant he'd fall into me.

His steely eyes grew wider, as the fire between us promised to consume us both. He focused on me as I studied him. I, his adoring voyeur, watched him edging closer to Eden.

He threw his head back, lashes fluttering for the moment before he plummeted into bliss. The last ebbs of desire that left his body came with parted perfect lips, and a whispered,
"I love you."

HE – DRIP

The heated air between us sizzles despite the smothering snow beyond the open curtains. No burning fireside required. No coals to match our own.

The bedroom wavers amidst our tempest, like the shimmering air above a racetrack. This world stands distorted. My eyes are only for you.

Somewhere, a clock ticks, or chimes, or screams for us to stop. But I can't. And I won't. And neither will you.

Silk on silk, skin on skin, we ease against each other. Not much. Just enough. We feel the sparks electrify our wanton lips.

Where are we? What are we doing? Is it wrong? The thoughts come thick and fast, but not as fast as these heavy breaths. *Just breathe. Just breathe.*

. . .

I'm lost in a world made by you, for you, in a universe only we inhabit. One in which the stars are your eyes and ethereal moonlight smears your skin. One of welcome, painless peace.

And through it all, through the pleasure and the pain, the ecstasy and exultation, all I can do, all I want to do, is watch you... drip.

SHE – FRUITS

Your lips provide respite, the peaks offering cover from the storm around us.
The words you speak are breaks in the clouds after years of sullen flooding. Prose of uttered pleasure become radiant pure light, slicing fog down the middle of these dreary days.
Splay me open and let the sun in.
Sustain the soil of my body, plant in me all your dreams.
Inches deep, lay the seed, I want all of you. The ugly, the rotten, the insane, the sorrow, your pain.
Sow in all your darkness and I will make fertile this alchemy and create for you pure joy.
No more will you search for the reckoning of understanding, nor the longing for peace.
The love I have for you fruits, find the nourishment you seek in me. Fore I am all things you'll ever need to feed your soul.

HE – SKIN ON SKIN

Wear me
Pull me on tight
Slip us together
Skin on skin
Sin on sin
Life on life
No need for tying
No need for knots
Time-measured perfection
Fluid as blood
No wrinkles
No creases
No reasons to weep
Melded, our atoms
Lovers
Soulmates
Us
We're touching already
Skin on skin

SHE – COGNAC

He bites his bottom lip with velveteen cognac deliberation, the tip of his tongue mulling over hills and valleys of pouting skin.

When I see his teeth rake over that lip it causes a supernova explosion inside my chest. I could disintegrate into a million stars and float into the atmosphere, like embers reaching for oxygen.

He says he wants to hold me gently, kiss me slowly. Worship me as the pious do when adoring angels; breathe me in to make his sweetest memory.

That's all lovely but this desire moves me differently...

I want him frenzied, like animals in heat.

Tear my flimsy cotton dress, bend me over the kitchen sink. Take me.

Wildly!

I need him to swallow me down with those dusky, ravenous eyes, then devour me like I'll be the last thing he'll ever consume. I'm hungry for him to bite into my tender flesh, 'Mark' my thighs with his mouth's moniker.

Wildly!

I'm desperate for him to net my raven tresses in his fist. Pull my hair like long marionette strings; he con-

trols me. I'm crazy for him to push me down on my knees whilst he sets the speed. Scream my name, empty his smooth cognac into me. I'm love drunk off his sex and poetry.
Wildly!

HE - WILD

Wild like the prairie
Eyes ablaze with the dawn
She prowls with the coyotes
Windswept hair and whip lashes
Taming the devil

Wild like the landscape
Fingernails scraping out a life
Oblivious to the dangers
Of snake, spider and worse
She's strong, so strong

Wild like the tempest
Blowing from altitudes high
Leaving the unprotected breathless
For scavengers to rape
Though never her

Wild like the snowstorm
Skin like moonshine blazing
Piercing ice with hazel glares
The winter cannot chill
A heart that beats an inferno

Wild like a forever
Where the sky glows indigo
And destiny shines a purple hue
Boundless clouds her destination
As she brings the prairie to me

SHE – IN BLACK

He was too hard to resist today,
All in black, with a brooding heart to match.
Sketching me with furrowed brow and rosy cheeks.
Shading lines in my face whilst I touched myself
underneath the sheets.

My love for him comes in commanding waves,
Building a crescendo of heat between my legs.

He was too hard to resist today,
My hips thrusting upward,
Reaching for him,
This heaven wrapped in the perfect body of a man.

I channel him through my fingers.
I have him this way 'til the moment I truly can.

HE – SMOKE AND MIRRORS

Smoke in her eyes
Blown in by life
Squinting with disappointments
She wipes them all away

Now, she stands
Proud and bold
Looking in the mirror
Eyes wide and wondrous

Not alone anymore
The ghost on her shoulder
Whispers the truth —
She's so very special

These moments are hers
To keep and to cherish
Until the mirror cracks
And he steps from the smoke

Taken in his arms
She'll sigh a contentment
As the lips on her neck
Whisper her name

SHE – UNDERGROUND RAVE

The nature of our chemistry plays out in the
beautiful length of his carotid artery.
It pulses parallel to hard music in underground
raves.
Staccato tympanic.
Light show static, like the gray intergalactic of
his dilated eyes.
Take another hit of me, the Ecstasy.
Ultrasonic reverberation in a primal rhythm.
I'm the one controlling the stick…
that keeps the tempo.
Wet my lips and dance for him, like that
throbbing vein under his skin.
Moving in sync to the pounding bass.
Circulatory symphonies echoing in his ears.
Heart beating, sweat dripping, blood
pumping just for me.
Underneath that length of drumming flesh.

HE – SHE BREAKS

She crashes upon my ragged cliffs,
like broken shells upon the beach,
her eyes speaking of tempests,
her maelstrom lips, out of reach.

We writhe together, she and I,
in this our private sea, striving
to compensate for that which we lack
namely, she and me.

SHE – HONEY DRIPPING

Sleep soundly pretty baby and when you dream, dream of me,

'fore the love I feel is deeper than the bottom of the sea.

I'm your wild mountain flower and you,

my English bumblebee.

We complement each other and make sweet honey

dripping

sugar

lines,

like freshly hung washing in the breeze.

I long to be the everything that brings you to your knees.

Seep me in your favorite cup, and I will be your tea,

then sip my heady flavor before you hit the sheets.

And I will lull you into resting where us lovers always meet.

In the land of wink and slumber, two souls with one heartbeat.

HE – RORSCHACH

Every twist and distortion
Every sweeping shadow
Every blot, spot, and smudge
Is her. Always her.
Her!

SHE – NATURE

He told me to write a poem about nature, of sweet peas and bluebell breezes that lift the hem of thin cotton dresses.

But our love story is of the darkness on this prairie. The kind that's brazen enough to endure.

We are the night hunting coyotes, grappling with the land to quell this hunger for one another.

Nothing can stop our love, this insatiable desire. We roam, searching, howling at the moon.

Can you hear me? Take what's yours, fight for me. Teeth bared and ready for battle, we do what it takes to sustain this need. Not miles, nor perils can impede us.

HE – ENTWINED

Move with me
Be my parasite
Stretch about this frame
And engorge
Devour this soul
Entwine, so tight
As to strangle
Force us together
So we might cling
Like ivies
Expanding as one
Until we wither
The same

THEY – PEAS

Two peas in a pod

Soft flesh against soft flesh

But no longer… green

THEY – FULLY IMMERSED

They slip beneath the waves of *them*
Dipped, doused, immersed
Swimming through eternity
Exploring each other's depths

THEY – MATHAMAGICS

$1 + 1 = $ *They*
Never a 2 for them
In an enforced solitaire
Of prohibited multiplications
And inward expansion,
Dividing into each other –
a magical singularity –
This perfect equation of *Us*

PART VII

LONGING

"To know and to want without ever the hope one might. This is the melancholy that seeps upon the lovers' souls when the moon rises high on one and the sun sets on the other. Time spares blushes but heaps misery upon the heart. To see. To touch. To feel. A second together's not too much to ask, is it?"

SHE – MY DARLING

My darling...Take me to the places you loved before I existed to you, before pain and happenstance tarnished the gleam in your eye.

Bring me to the riverbank where it flooded that day. Let's play in the waterspouts while the cantankerous rabbits hunker down to watch us laugh. Be silly with me, I long to see your joy.

Show me your comic books, we'll fall into the world of superheroes and villains. Read me your favorites, like chapters from sacred texts. I want to Marvel at the universe those pages create for you.

Deliver me to that abbey in the crumbling castle by the sea. Let me worship at your feet, pray you with gentle palm against your holy flesh. Take from my body, exult me above all things. I need you to love me, like I'm your religion.

HE – COME TO ME

Come to me
For my needs are greater than theirs

Come to me
For the oceans shall part before our love

Come to me
Even if the stars should fall and block your path

Come to me
So the universe might realign

Come to me
So this heart won't feel so lost

Come to me
My angel, my darling, my everything

Come to me
Just come

SHE – CLASSIC RED LIPSTICK

My love…your smile is always lighting up my thoughts,
like fireflies bobbing in dusky southern gloaming.
It's the sweetness of that smile I adore most of your face.
I must confess every-time I see your mouth I'm thinking…
I want you to kiss me hard,
like Scarlett O'Hara and Rhett.
Swept back into disoriented bliss.
Don't hold back, smear my classic red lipstick.
Take all from me, be eager and greedy.
Like my mouth will be the last thing you ever taste,
insatiable and starving.
Consume me.
I want to feel your coarse beard stubble against my delicate skin.
Kiss me hard till my mouth is swollen and ripe,
Again
And
Again
And
Again

HE – CLOSE ENOUGH TO TOUCH

She sits beside me close enough to touch. If I breathe too deeply, we will. I hear her sigh as my fingers fly across the keyboard, as if with a will of their own. In truth, they have, as my mind, like my eyes, lie elsewhere.

Time passes in a perfect silence. She watches and learns. I learn as she watches. There are moments when I think the sofa may give, that the soft, worn leather will dip and she will tip against me. Our legs will brush, trouser to skirt, with the wish of skin on skin. Her flesh will goose-pimple and she'll giggle like the girl she once was, and to me, still is.

I don't realise I've typed 'The End' until she sits back and puffs out her cheeks. Her face is flush with fresh roses in the summer. Her eyes twinkle like dewdrops in the spring. There is a winter blizzard blazing in her heart. I feel it. When the autumn rises in her lips, I fall.

. . .

"Me?" she asks, pointing at the words on the screen.

"Always," I answer, without even seeing what they say.

Our legs touch, as do our lips.

SHE – WHO IS HE?

He's like snow in July
Firecracker fountains falling from the sky
Droplets of water in desert fever dreams
The double stitch anchors when I'm ripping at the seams.

HE – HER ARCHITECTURE

A study in perfection, she exudes
Femininity,
Lust,
Seduction,
Wrapped around love's tongue
Like words from a poet's quill.
Ink staining pure veins blue,
Her architecture delivers wonders
Beyond the sculpted cheekbones
And lips of pouting seductions.
It delivers
Her mind,
Her heart,
Her soul.
She is what she will always be
To he who paints her in delicacies:
The object grey eyes fall upon
In both pleasure and pain.
She is this and more, his siren,
Raven-haired and hazel eyes,
Undiminished by time and by life:
His waking dream,
And always shall be.

SHE - WATER SPORTS

My darling…
Take me to the places you loved before I existed to you.
Before pain and happenstance tarnished the gleam in your eye.
Bring me to the riverbank where it flooded that day.
Let's play in the waterspouts,
while cantankerous rabbits hunker down to watch us laugh.
Be silly with me,
I long to see your joy.

HE – FROSTED FLOWER

Frosted flower, iced crust to velvet soft, she sparkles. Oh, how she sparkles before all others.

Frosted flower, too delicate to touch, she glistens. Oh, how she glistens through her web of gossamer tears.

Frosted flower, preserved like a diamond, she gleams. Oh, how she gleams through this false, polished night.

Frosted flower, never meant for a vase in a nondescript room, she shivers. Oh, how she shivers herself apart.

Frosted flower, girl in the corner, she trembles. Oh, how she trembles at the touch to come.

Frosted flower, the one with no name, don't leave. Oh, don't leave and defy my hesitation.

Frosted flower, ever in my eyes, shining. Oh, how her memory blinds me always.

SHE – SKIN

I look at him every Tuesday, sweat sliding down his stomach, lungs heaving heavy against his bird cage chest.

Bone and tendon protecting the lonely heart pounding beneath it.

I am ravenous to be the towel that pats him dry and wraps him in the knowing that I was born for only that task.

My fibrous matter licks away the beads of salty perspiration, one drop at a time until there is an ocean of him inside me.

I am the cause of his gooseflesh friction; I shall make my home in the tiny, landscaped mounds on his dermis.

To be those midnight jeans that press against him, hugging the sinew wrapped around the taut muscles of his thighs.

Let me take care of that button fly.

Wear me, drape me across your flesh. I will be your finest garb when you want to look your best.

HE – AQUALUNG

Breathe for me, I'm drowning

                                        Airless without you

Pump life into this heart

                                        I'm gasping, like a fish

Born without gills but

                                        Still craving the ocean

Pour yourself upon me

                                        Be my oxygen,

Carry me to such depths

                                        Submerge me in darkness

Allow your luminescence

                                        To light the way

As I draw my everything

                         From your lungs

SHE – TWINKLING LIGHTS

Words spoken between us transpose like sound waves,
Vibrating on a golden wire, connecting our souls.
My darling…we made love for hours today, like the tide languidly rolling away from Whitby's shore,
Cresting and crashing together again and again until we were one.
I bend with you, becoming the coaxing curves of your glorious smile.
Slip into me and speak in ardent tongue, a locution like my heart has never known before.
Let your fingertips dip into the clouds that swirl around my mind, as you sentiently slide into twilight.
You behold my face, adamantly memorizing me,
Gazing with those gray eyes, like you're watching twinkling lights through frosted windowpanes at Christmas.
I see myself glowing in them and pray, I always radiate that way for you.

HE – ALMOST

She swims the ventricle streams of his heart,
like a salmon returning home after years in the
wilderness.
He accepts this return without fear of intrusion.
The spawning is almost upon them.
Almost…
Souls split apart always reunite.
They pull towards each other through time and space,
solidity and thought, striving to undo the cosmic
bridges dividing them.
The rainbow conjunction is as inevitable as that final
perfect night into which they'll descend.
Almost…
There is a moment where eyes meet, hearts sync, skin
touches.
One before. One after.
These two lovers who were always meant to be, exist in
the prelude to both.
Tongues flicker in anticipation.
Eyes grow wide.
Skin radiates.
Almost…

Almost… there.

THEY – SKIN ON SKIN

They lie together, skin on skin, listening to the sounds of each other's hearts. Two slivers of golden light, one the early afternoon sun, the other a new dawn, reveal their faces like the first new day in Eden. There is nothing else to disturb their meeting. Divided by two thin layers of glass, the four thousand miles that severs their holding each other seem so little yet so far. They are one, in their way, or wish to be. They always were.

There is no need for words. No requirement to impress. Soulmates born and bred, they have found each other, wishing for nothing other than to stare deep into each other's eyes. There is no hiding from each other, and they don't want to.

One of them blinks, dispelling the steel he has had to garner, melting away into black pools of darkness, a midnight shade he would share if she'll let him. In response, she smiles. This is all he's ever wanted.

The beauty responds by batting eyelashes she would normally hide behind layers of makeup and serene defences. He sees through it, though. There, living in twin glades of tortoiseshell, sometimes tipping into brown, other times, a lush green, her irises also darken as if in response to his own.

They stare at each other. They often stare. There is

no need for words and never has been. Only when they wish to talk, do they. Lips part to dilating pupils, perhaps dreaming of more, and they lose themselves in tales told, of youth, and mistakes, and experiences now shared. Their lives have been so different, circles lived and almost fulfilled. But at the zenith of these arcing stories, they close upon each other as links of a chain waiting to be sealed about each other. They are so close. The bonds are unbreakable.

They care so much. Too much. The same pain and heartache are experienced by both. What one feels, the other grinds upon. What one experiences, the other tastes and touches. She smiles again, and he is lost.

There are moments when she brushes her lips with pale, sender fingertips that he thinks he might die. The sensations of love overwhelm him. He knows nothing of such things. Only when he looks into those eyes once more, falls into the wells of her soul, does he see she, too, is lost.

They reach for each other and hold on tight. Soulmates who have found themselves despite all that time and life and God has set between them, they cling to their love with talon-like tenacity. To remove one from the other would shred reality: This is how much they love each other.

'Soon,' she whispers. 'Heart to heart and skin to skin.'

He pictures it in his mind's eye, slipping in beside her, looking into her soul. He sees that same smile. That same changing of colour in her skin, eyes, aura. And there it is, that promise of a lightened eternity, where they walk hand in hand and make love beneath the stars at will.

Forever lasts a long time once it's reached. It's the minutes before which are the hardest to walk.

PART VIII

HOPES & POSSIBILITIES

"There is what, will, what might, and what must be. The former two are obvious to all, from friends to family and everyone in-between. The latter, now, these are only known to the lovers. They feel them so strongly that all else amalgamates, as 'They' slip into eternity together."

THEY - OTHER WORLDS

She – Poe

Born first to the authors, fittingly at the stroke of midnight.

When he came into the world, he didn't utter a sound like most newborn infants do.

He was above such nonsense.

Instead, he looked long at all he had known many times before.

In his cobalt eyes there was always a deep reckoning.

He nuzzled deep against his mother's breast to hear her familiar heartbeat and was delighted to realize he was a wish made real.

Pale skin, sooty hair, and raven sensibilities, he brooded and thought deeply like his father.

Hand cupping his temple as he pondered over the queries of life.

The microcosms of multiplying atoms, the supernovas of exploding space.

All whirling around under those lazy curls.

Poe the conundrum.

Athletic and strong, flying down the rugby pitch as if on the wings of eagles.

Also, soft, and pensive. Those penetrating eyes soaking up the beauty of twilight, he was never afraid to weep at the sight of such glory.

The envy of his friends. The idolatry of the girls, he could've had his pick of anyone. They hung on his words like ripe cherries offering up their sweetnesses.

Still, he waited staunchly and quietly. Holding out for a love like the one that created him. Proof that storybook endings and fate existed, just as the crow flies. He was certain his heart would find its way home.

He – Brontë

I'd have wanted her to look like her mother, our unborn daughter, raven hair long and luxurious, eyes like a waking dream, skin like snow.

We'd have called her Brontë. I think she'd have liked that, a literary tilt to a beauty which began from a love of words.

Her hair would have whipped about her as we strode across the moors, her mother's hand in mine as we worshipped the wild nature. How we'd have laughed.

I'd have given my heart for that daughter made real, as I have for her mother since that day. Oh, that day! When passion became too much, and love linked our souls. I'd have told Brontë that story every night as her mother enveloped her in front of the fire before I carried them both to bed.

But Brontë and her siblings are a life lived elsewhere, somewhere, or still to come. The legacy of her would-have-been parents, however, that will continue until they find her.

I love you...
Both x

She – Silvia

The baby, Silvia. The surprise, Silvia. Her spirit raged to existence from exploding stardust. The tiny creature was brought to earth like a comet crashing into the world. Beautiful, awe inspiring and yes, more than a bit overwhelming.

The authors had her late in life, Silvia was sent to keep them on their toes. She whirled around the house like the dust-devil that wrapped around her father when he was a boy. Much like that mini tornado, Silvia wouldn't be forgotten or ignored.

The last of the bunch always turns out differently. The three other children before had features like their mother. Pale complexion with ebon hair. Silvia came out British. Curly honey-colored locks, peaches and cream skin. Her looks were deceiving, she often time would be mistaken for a heavenly cherub. Everyone in the family surmised that she indeed was from the other direction.

'Silvia! Did you paint the cat!?'
'Silvia! You do not jump off the roof!'
'SILVIA!'

The authors could be heard up and down the seaside wailing her name. The neighbours would smirk, knowing that she was a combination of everything obnoxious and gauche about each of her parents.

Silvia's tongue was quick and glib like both her mother and father. She was a tiny cobra watching from the reeds. Recording people's weaknesses and unsavory attributes, it was only during formal dinners or meaningful holidays when she'd strike. The smarts would flow from her cupie-bow lips like Niagara Falls. The onslaught wasn't over until she made someone blush or cry. Her mother would raise one eyebrow and look at her father with a scowl.

'Control your child.'

Her father would look at little Silvia with a gleam in his eye and slyly wink in her direction.

He – William

His words pour across the tabletop like rain from
  the clouds, nourishing.
Lives measured in the sparkling stars of eyes and
  white, crescent moon smiles.
His is the talent poured from his mother's
  daring heart and his father's will.
His is the courage spawned of parents prepared
  to say no, so he didn't have to.
The bard of the band. The wordsmith of the
  thinkers and his creative siblings,
We'd have called him William, because like his
  mother, he'd have been incomparable.

THEY – GENERATIONAL

PART 1 – The Niece

He lay worn and frail in the home he'd lived in for his whole adult life. The floorboards creaked and groaned like the rusty joints resting under his flesh. This old man visited delirium, flying in and out of reality to call on places of his past. He was close, with one foot in this world and the other dangling on the edge of eternity.

He had outlived them all. Staved off death by making it his star. Every novel, every poem, an ode to the grave. The endless love letters to the reaper bought him nearly 100 years of heart beats. Even the stars burn out though, and time always comes to collect its due.

'Hello, Uncle.'

The man opened his cobalt eyes to peer at the sweet face of his niece. Age had not marred the apples of her cheeks or the twinkle in her impish gaze. Her wheat-colored hair grazed his brow as she leaned over to hug him.

A moment of clarity washed over the old man. He smiled at her and gave a wink. His niece never failed to visit every Sunday, despite being a grandmother who was busy with a family of her own.

'How are you feeling, Uncle? Are you well enough to tell me a good tall tale today? Can you spin me a yarn?'

The man nodded and cleared his throat before speaking. He let his eyes flutter up to the ceiling and began.

'Once upon a time there was a love so pure and beautiful that most would believe it to be a fairy tale. It was a love that was boundless. Miles couldn't separate, nor circumstance could break it. It was a love that gave grace to people who were most hard on themselves.'

'Two individuals that were not perfect, but so perfect for one another that there was no space between them. One heart, one vow and one mind governed their joined consciousness.'

He took an easier breath. Oh, the bliss and excitement it gave him to tell the story.

'The girl had only come to visit once. One visit was all that was needed to change his life forever. She was a foreigner to England, and possibly earth. An angel so sweet that the cruelties of most circumstances were too harsh for her tender heart to bare. Yet she endured, never really knowing happiness or peace. Her eyes alone spoke of the chasm inside her chest where all her hardships settled.'

He was determined to lift her burdens, so he became her best friend first. He lived to make her happy. Jokes to make her giggle, daily tasks to remind her of how important she was. It wasn't until that one ordinary day in autumn during their brief time together, when he found out how life was really meant to be lived.

'The daft girl she was, thought it would be exciting to take the bus to see the earth rotating in church.'

His niece looked up from her needlepoint. Her forehead furrowed in concern. 'The earth rotating in church?' The old man must have lost lucidity again.

'Uncle, I'll give you some pain medicine so you can rest.'

The old man dismissed the suggestion with a

shooing hand. He carried on more urgently, as the words to his story stumbled out of his mouth.

'He watched her looking at the scenery on that bus ride. Many a day he had taken that same route, past the same countryside. However, studying her face as she took everything in was like he, himself was a newborn seeing the light for the first time. He viewed everything afresh through her kaleidoscope eyes. She was so warm and inviting, he could feel the curves of her thigh pressing against his, in that shared bus seat. He was grateful for that confined form of transportation. It allowed him to touch his dream.'

His niece aided him with a sip of water. It felt good to wet his parched mouth. He let the cool droplets absorb into his lips. It had been so long since he felt anything but the rim of a cup against them.

'They entered the dark sacred place together, shoulders touching as they walked through the holy doors of that ancient cathedral. So quiet and calm was the atmosphere that he would hear her draw a breath of wonderstruck air into her lungs.'

'There it stood, suspended in the ether above the baptismal font. The perfect pairing of religion and science, a hologram of the rotating earth.'

'It spun on an invisible axis as the light outside danced through the stain glass windows. Out of all the beautiful things God had created, the clouds, the sun, they paled in comparison to her looking up at the hologram globe twirling above them.'

He could feel the slowing down of his heart. Just enough time to finish the story. He removed a simple gold band that had grooved into his finger for decades. The old man continued the story as he placed the ring into his niece's palm.

'There they stood in holy silence. Him staring at her in awe, whilst she gazed upon the earth. She turned to look into his cobalt eyes and knew that all they had was then. Happiness and love in that moment. It radiated from them both. With peace and promise, she took off her ring and without saying a word placed it on his finger. A tear escaped from her feather lashes

and made a trail down her cheek. So moved by the gesture, he cupped her face to catch the tear and kiss her lips. As one, they seemed to float above it all, until the church and the earth grew smaller and smaller.'

'Wait Uncle, who does this ring belong to?' The old man's niece struggled to hold back tears as she knew her uncle's story was at its final page. He continued in a whisper.

'With that kiss they flew far away from worldly strife, the two bound by fate and love everlasting.'

'My dear niece, I see as clearly now as I could that day when I kissed her. Our love was the ascension into a heaven we made for one another. Higher and higher above that holographic orb until the only thing flooding my vision was a perfect 'Dot.''

His eyes closed for the last time as he thanked God for that autumn all those years ago.

PART 2 – The Granddaughter

"Who's Dot?"

Her granddaughter had found it deep within an old laptop's archive. A file labelled 'Dot's Diary - A Work of Fiction' if the thing had been real and not part of a micro-chip it would've held at least a foot of dust.

"Leave it," grumbled her grandma.

The granddaughter was a good girl, but she'd inherited a nose for nuisance, like her father, whose hacking skills, those honed first at college and then latterly the government's defence programme had caused no matter of mischief. If anything, she was even better than him, and no file that sparked an interest was keeping her out.

She sneaked the thing out into the yard, that which her grandmother had spent years creating. There, the moonflowers cast a pale glow across her mocha skin, as the roses rambled, and the irises reached for the sky.

She spent the next several hours immersed in reading, as her grandmother glowered down from the bedroom window through still strong eyes.

She read and read and read: Tales of Gaia, the North Sea, home. It was all there, every last word documented for posterity.

The girl returned to the bedroom much later. Her grandmother was waiting for her, cantankerous as ever, fists balled and mouth ready for battle. "How dare you!" She stopped as suddenly to as she'd started.

The girl was inconsolable. Her eyes bulged with tears, her cheeks red and skin wetted. She clutched the laptop close to her breast and stood there shaking her head. "It's the saddest story I've ever read," she eventually mustered. "Dot loved her Petal so much. It's not right they couldn't be together."

"True," nodded her grandmother. The old lady sighed an inhalation to turn a tide and settled back down on the pillow. Her chin jutted forward in grim determination, but her eyes betrayed her.

"It's you, isn't it. You're Dot." They weren't questions. She knew. The girl was just as powerful with observations as her grandmother.

"Yes."

"And Petal?"

The old woman looked away, her once ebony hair now streaked with silver and auburn that caught the last light of the day like molten metals. "I could never love a man more. I never have."

"I can tell," said her granddaughter, as she sat at the bottom of the bed. "Who was he? He wasn't a work of fiction that's for damn sure."

"Watch your mouth. No cussing in this house."

The girl sniffed back a grin, for her gran cussed nine times a minute. "So? Who was he, grandma? Please?"

She looked back as the last sunlight dipped to darkness and whispered, "Petal."

"Ooh, you haven't called me that in years." His cobalt eyes glowed a steely defiance, for the death his wife had predicated on them both for more decades than he cared to remember had still failed to materialise, bed-bound though they were.

"You're Petal. Then...?"

"She always was a sceptic. Still, I love her even more now than I did back then." He leaned over, difficult though it was, and planted a kiss on his wife's cheek."

"I prefer them on the lips," she retorted, a supernatural fire burning in her eyes.

"Like I said," said he, "sceptical and so very, very cantankerous. Best fiction writer the world's ever seen, though." He patted her hand, and she closed her fingers around his own. "I wish she'd let me publish it."

When the pair looked up, the night now full and time having passed in hours not minutes, their granddaughter had vanished. For sometimes, just sometimes, some peoples' love is so strong it's best left only to those entangled in it.

THEY – FOREVER

Once upon a time there was he
who was born to string words together on golden
threads.
He wrote and wished for a girl and 7 years later she was
born from his prose.
And for that she vowed to love him...

Forever

In a land far away, a dawn rose,
blasting away the darkness he cuddled so close.
She lived and breathed unknown to him, distant, yet
only a phone screen away,
And in knowing this he vowed to love her

Forever

Two children that would grow to more,
separated by tide and time and experience,
unfulfilled, they went through the motions of life in
search of more.
And eventually, they found it.

Forever

SHE – BUTTERFLY

She had paper-thin wings
Like wet party streamers
In summer rainstorms.

Disintegrated joy.

This butterfly curled in on herself.
She remembered that it was safer
In cocooned coffins.

Celebration cemeteries

Where the past was buried,
She prayed to slumber in a chrysalis grave
Convinced there was only death
And no respite from the weather.
Among the asphalt and soot, she landed,

Rock bottom

The butterfly waited to be taken
By elements unrelenting.
Her crepe sails weighted in despair,
Antennae hung low.
She had given up,
But it wasn't goodbye for her.

A miracle

Perhaps luck or God or a bit of both.
He arrived with the sun
In the nick of time,
A smile and a helping hand.
He picked her up,
Placed her to perch
And regain her strength
Launched from a steadfast palm.
Finally, she could
Spread her wings and fly.

Knowing

He loved her enough to let her soar.

HE – YOU FOUND ME

You found me hanging from chipped fingernails looking up, not down, unbothered by gravity. Your voice recalled this form, grasped the wrist, dragged my all across the precipice. I hadn't seen you, then, but I'd known you my entire life.

Life lifted from me like a veil. Or was it death? Colour dismissed the gloom, like a rainbow duster polishing away the night. Sounds returned. Warmth and comfort infused my soul. You did this to me. You.

We made our home upon that cliff, dressed it up in flowers and birdsong, worked this little patch of ours. And though no one knew us, and no one saw us, we were happy together. That's where they found us, you and me, locked in an eternal embrace.

SHE – PERENNIAL LOVE

In our next life, I hope we are bulbs planted in the same soil, our roots tangled deep in the earth.

In our next life, I know these stems will be strong. Each fanning petal blooming outward, under the sun of a shared future.

In our next life, we will drink of the rain. Nourishing a love so beautiful that all the world will gasp at our glory.

In our next life, the summer will end, and the wind will rage cold and bitter. We will wither together under the weight of first frost. Heads bowed low in prayer and quiet dormancy. Knowing the next spring we will flower for one another once more.

HE – THIS SOUL

I possess a soul,
One I no longer own.
I cannot give it,
Nor bequeath it,
For it is already hers,
She who is my ever-after,
To do with as she wishes,
As she does my heart.
Be gentle, my darling,
This soul,
The real me,
Is all I've ever owned.

SHE – YOU TELL ME

He whispered:
'My Beauty, how does it feel to know that someone cherishes you so much?'
I replied:
'You tell me.'

My Darling...you know my love has made you stronger. I am the elixir flowing its way into your body, mending all your broken parts.

I needle-eyed a strand of my hair to sew the torn tendons of your tired legs. For years you have tried to outrun your demons and self-doubt, sprinting faster as they licked at your heels. Will you ever glance over your shoulder? Stop running and realize you've beaten them.

You've won!

I am your prize at the finish line. Claim me!

My Darling...your heart was so sick when I met you. It beat in rhythm like footsteps on prison floors.

'Dead man walking!'

Then I came along, offered you reprieve on those death sentence blues. I doctored your heart with salve from my own.

No longer caged, live, breathe. Be free with me.

My Darling...when I found you, your mind was so dark. The loneliness cast shadows in your eyes, like storm clouds during a prairie squall. The melancholy of your thoughts endlessly rolling in upturned anguish.

I couldn't bear the torment.

So, I opened my consciousness and showed you my pondering, twin minds split from one atom. You needn't worry about being alone. Wherever your musings wander, mine go too.

You are finally understood.

My Darling...don't you see? I've given you all of me, so you always know what it feels like to be cherished.

HE – SMALL SPACES

My wish?
To share a small space with you.
Somewhere tight, compact, where we lie close.
So close, in fact, our lips press tight,
Our bodies, skin on skin, dissolving together.
Those areas ordinarily caged, not.
Preferably a somewhere dark, unseen,
Beyond the reach of the revealing light.
Hidden far from prying eyes,
Secure.
Yes, a small space big enough for one,
Yet prized for two.
So, I beg you, my always, my darling, my dream,
Die with me, so we might share an eternal coffin,
And never know the agony of *this* again.

THEY – TISSUE PAPER HEARTS

Her heart, a tissue paper poppy, painted crimson, delicately blooming, straining against worldly winds that seek to rip her away. Scented with the lifeblood of the prairie, born for azure days and citrine rays, she wafts an ethereal dream through his wandering mind.

There are many flowers in the grasslands, poking their heads above the rippling emerald and gold waves, striving, but only one such as she. Beauty is in the eye of the beholder they claim, but she is the only beauty his eye has ever seen; such paradoxes entwine their love.

To pick her is to end her. To cup her is to stifle the strength she exudes. Yet his eyes are upon her, this flash of colour in a subdued world of many. A vermillion supernova in the ebony night, a ruby coral beneath the aquamarine sea, his poppy shall bloom eternally deep within his obsidian heart.

They say she's not real, this tissue paper dream, this reluctant flower, this beautiful girl. But he sees her, wants her, needs her, and in no asylum is he: *She must be real. Must be.* So as the prairie nourishes, he must nourish. And he shall. For to know her is to love her and love her he does. They are bound.

Hearts and flowers. Flowers and hearts. Prairie, wilderness, grasslands, or just a waking dream. He thinks. He loves. He cherishes. *Like a raincloud*, she says. There are worse things to be. For he shall rise forever above her, and she shall always lay beneath him petals unfurled.

THEY – 8TH NEW WONDER OF THE WORLD

There are many extraordinary things in life. Sights, places, experiences, that cause such a movement in the soul that one would compare them to paradise. An Eden of enigmatic inspiration and awe. Seven New Wonders that take your breath away, leave a print on your heart and a promise that they will linger in you for a lifetime.

First New Wonder of the World. The Colosseum filled with warriors fighting for sport whilst the blood lusting crowds gathered to see exhausted downfall. Two brave titans enter, only one knew he'd leave. Risking it all to survive lives that they were born into. Destiny's despair, to be raised as pawns for battles impossible to win. Death or guilt is the trophy for entrapment.

Second New Wonder of the World. The Great Wall of China built to withstand siege from the perils of an unforgiving war. This labor of land and loyalty, two millennia long, remains impermeable from outside influences that mean to destroy the treasures behind it. Nothing can break through. Not an army with a thousand swords, nor the furious elements of nature can crumble it.

Third New Wonder of the World. The Taj Mahal, an alabaster tomb erected in opulent observance. A monumental grief, so long and deep that the great emperor could not rest until his muse had a marble chamber to spend her endless sleep. All the beauty she possessed in life, the great emperor would design for her in death. Clean white walls and crisp mosaics echo of time spent together. Memories too beautiful to let go, are entombed for eternity, because adoration and fate never die. Immortal mortar.

Fourth New Wonder of the World. Christ the Redeemer. He looks down from high atop a mountain, at those who believe and those who want to. He knows God is in us and all around us. Faith gives us shelter, hope has us endure one more day. Christ the Redeemer sees heaven on earth as I see heaven in you.

Fifth New Wonder of the World. Manchu Picchu, the lost city of the Incas. Were their lives like ours? What tawdry details weaved their existence together? Did they quarrel, laugh, tell jokes? What mass exodus drove them away from a life that was only ordinary? Did they have the reckoning that something better was just beyond the horizon? Could it be they abandoned the past to get there?

Sixth New Wonder of the World. At ChichenItza, they were willing to sacrifice it all to worship their deities. A devotion so pure one would be the offering, held down under the glare of the midday sun. Splayed chest and eager heart, take of the flesh to appease.

Seventh New Wonder of the World. Petra housed sacred libraries. Poems of ponder and prose, papyrus pages laid in stacks. Were there scribes trying to capture emotion like we do? Ancient alphabets written of longing and loss, trial and triumph. Nothing has changed, same stories in different centuries. Since the beginning of time, we all want the same thing...to be seen, heard, and understood by those we hold dear.

Eighth New Wonder of the World...*Our love...*

THEY – A QUESTION TUCKED AWAY

'Why me? Of all the men. Why me?'

He asks the question that haunts him *when* he's alone in the dark. Desperate riddles screamed silently into pillows that don't spill secrets. Is he afraid I'll see the vulnerability in his eyes? He doesn't want to show me the restless boy churning inside the man he had to be. I know that boy, anyway. The one that hides under duvets to avoid the monsters called reality and rejection.

You ask: *'Why me?'*

Does the stem of a cherry blossom ask its fruiting labors *'Why?'* when they grow together? No, they just exult in the glory of love and photosynthesis. Does the paper that houses these words asks the pen why it scribbles? It doesn't, it simply lays beneath the quill like frozen water reflections, all the while welcoming cursive letter 'I love yous' as they pirouette across the page.

. . .

The boy in you wants to know *'Why?'*

Tuck him in tight. Put him in bed and tell him the story of how I chose love. Like the tree and quill, I knew there was more magic in *'Us'* together.

THEY – AFTERWORD

"Never, The End."

ABOUT THE AUTHORS

Gina Maria Manchego is a mixed-medium author and artist from the beautiful state of Colorado, USA. Gina is deeply influenced by the vastness of the prairie where she's made her home, every wildflower and colossal skyscape echo in the work she creates.

When Gina Maria is not busy with her art and words, she can be found spending time with her lovely teenage son. Together, they enjoy discussing filmography, history and taking walks.

Gina Maria has dedicated much of her life to advocacy and social work. She has been fortunate to lend her expertise in writing, and multi-medium creativity to help others through art therapy.

Gina Maria was fortunate enough to have her first written work published when she was eighteen years old. Since then, she's been honored to be published in many tremendous magazines and journals, such as: Gobblers and Masticadores, Lothlorien Poetry Journal, Dark Winter Literary Magazine, Flora Fiction, Impspired Literary Magazine, and Skyway Journal.

Gina is also a Spillwords Literary Press featured author.

Gina Maria's lifetime goal is to spend her days creating meaningful stories and artistry that can move one's soul. She can be found on Twitter/X: @GiUknit and WordPress: ginamanchegoauthor@wordpress.com

Richard M. Ankers is a native of the beautiful county of Yorkshire, England. When Richard isn't writing, he can be found running, keeping fit, or drinking coffee with his friends. If he could write in full view of the mountains with a stream running past his garden, he'd probably never resurface. He has four published novels to his name: The Eternals, Hunter Hunted, Into Eternity, (all part of The Eternals Series) and Britannia Unleashed. Richard is a former Gold Medal winner on Authonomy.com by HarperCollins with his novel The Snow Lily. He has appeared in many anthologies including The Clockwork Chronicles, Love Letters To Poe: Volume 1, Once Upon A Broken Dream and Clockwork Christmas. Richard has featured in magazines worldwide such as DailyScienceFiction, Bunbury Magazine, Expanded Field Journal, Spillwords, and always feels privileged to do so. He counts himself fortunate to have over fifty writing credits to his name from his decade in writing. Richard also now writes with his co-author Gina Maria Manchego. When people ask why he writes, he simply replies: 'Because I have to'.

Richard can be found on Twitter/X at: @Richard_Ankers, and on his blog at: richardankers.com, as well as in Next Chapter's website at https://nextchapter.pub/authors/richard-ankers-gothic-fantasy-author

The Poetry of Pronouns
ISBN: 978-4-82418-818-2
Mass Market

Published by
Next Chapter
2-5-6 SANNO
SANNO BRIDGE
143-0023 Ota-Ku, Tokyo
+818035793528

20th October 2023

www.ingramcontent.com/pod-product-compliance
Lightning Source LLC
LaVergne TN
LVHW032010070526
838202LV00059B/6382